no strangers

ancient wisdom in a modern world

**ANNENBERG SPACE
FOR PHOTOGRAPHY**

First Published in the United States of America by

Annenberg Space for Photography
2000 Avenue of the Stars, Los Angeles, CA 90067
tel: 213.403.3000 | fax: 213.403.3100 | annenbergspaceforphotography.org

ISBN 978-0-9884659-0-9

Design: Brand Navigation
Cover Image: © Randy Olson, OlsonFarlow.com

no strangers

ancient wisdom in a modern world

Annenberg Space for Photography

Written by Wade Davis, Ph.D.

Explorer-in-Residence, National Geographic Society

Photo: © Chris Rainier

ANNENBERG SPACE
FOR PHOTOGRAPHY

no
strangers

ancient wisdom in a modern world

" The ideal of a single civilization for everyone, implicit in the

cult of progress and technique, impoverishes and mutilates us.

Every view of the world that becomes extinct, every culture

that disappears, diminishes a possibility of life. "

—OCTAVIO PAZ

contents

no strangers shines a light on rare and indigenous peoples – communities that can seem stunning in their simplicity, other-worldly in their ritualistic beauty. As first-class photojournalism, these breathtakingly-captured, carefully-curated images are enlightening, uplifting, essential. As pure aesthetic expression, they stand with the very best of modern art.

But look into the eyes of the subjects themselves. Then look even deeper. At the pride and the frailty, the joy and the isolation, the underlying and undeniable humanity that would be as much at home in corporate board meeting as in a tribal ceremony.

I am deeply proud that we are able to present these works, to support those who chronicle cultures that are rapidly changing, and shrinking – for reasons good and bad, justifiable and inexplicable. But while we must preserve and document these cultures, we must also recognize the mirror they provide us – to see our own essential selves – to see the laughing, crying, caring beings we all are – regardless of where we live or the culture we inhabit.

WALLIS ANNENBERG
Chairman of the Board, President and CEO of the Annenberg Foundation

As our distant ancestors set out from Africa, they walked through desert sands and over snow-covered passes, through jungles and mountain streams, eventually finding their way across oceans and coral atolls to the beaches of unknown continents. Along the way they invented ten thousand different ways of being.

Over the last decade geneticists have proved a philosopher's dream to be true. We are all brothers and sisters. Studies of the human genome have left no doubt that the genetic endowment of humanity is a single continuum. Race is an utter fiction. We are all cut from the same genetic cloth, descendants of a relatively small number of individuals who walked out of Africa some 60,000 years ago. On a subsequent journey that lasted 40,000 years, some 2,500 generations carried the human spirit to every corner of the habitable world.

But here is the important and revelatory idea. If all of humanity emerged from the same primordial fountain of life, all cultures share essentially the same mental acuity, the same raw genius. Whether this intellectual capacity and potential is exercised in stunning technological innovations, as has been the great achievement of the West, or by untangling the complex threads of memory inherent in a myth — a primary concern, for example, of the Aborigines of Australia — is simply a matter of choice and orientation, adaptive insights and cultural priorities.

There is no hierarchy of progress in the history of culture, no Social Darwinian ladder to success. The Victorian notion of the savage and the civilized,

Photo: © Randy Olson, OlsonFarlow.com

Photo: © Steve McCurry/Magnum Photos

Photo: © Angela Fisher & Carol Beckwith

Photo: © Angela Fisher & Carol Beckwith

with European industrial society sitting proudly at the apex of a pyramid of advancement that rises from a base of so-called primitives, has been thoroughly discredited — indeed, scientifically ridiculed for the racial and colonial conceit that it was. The brilliance of scientific research and the revelations of modern genetics have affirmed in an astonishing way the essential connectedness of humanity.

We share a sacred endowment, a common history written in our bones. It follows, as this exhibition suggests, that the myriad cultures of the world are not failed attempts at modernity, let alone failed attempts to be us. They are unique expressions of the human imagination and heart, unique answers to a fundamental question: What does it mean to be human and alive? When asked this question, the cultures of the world respond in 7,000 different voices that compose our human repertoire for dealing with all the challenges that will confront us as a species over the next 2,500 generations, even as we continue this never-ending journey.

circle of life

All peoples face the same adaptive imperatives. We all must give birth to our children, raise, educate and protect them, and console our elders in their final years. Virtually all cultures would endorse most tenets of the Ten Command-ments, not because the Judaic world was uniquely inspired, but because it articulated rules that allowed a social species to thrive. Few societies fail to outlaw murder or thievery. All create traditions that bring order to marriage and procreation. Every culture honors its dead, even as it struggles with the separation that death implies.

We all draw from a universal well of emotions. Everyone knows the wonder of joy, the agony of sorrow, the promise of hopes and dreams. Everywhere the sharing of food is the fulcrum of daily life, love of family the foundation of society, gift exchange and trade the symbols of the reciprocal entanglement of relationships that woven together create the fabric of civilization.

 All peoples face the same adaptive imperatives.

All draw from a universal well of emotions.

Every culture has defined notions of proper etiquette, gestures of grace and kindness that smooth human interactions. And everywhere one encounters the quest for the divine, and a reflexive desire to elevate the spirit through the embrace of some technique of ecstasy, be it prayer, dance, the pain of ordeal or the ingestion of sacred plants.

Given all that we have in common, the range and diversity of our cultural adaptations are astonishing. Hunting and gathering societies have flourished from the rain forests of Southeast Asia and the Amazon to the deserts of Australia, from the Kalahari to the icy reaches of the Arctic, from the American plains to the pampas of Patagonia. Wayfarers and fishermen have settled nearly every island chain in all the world's oceans. Complex societies have been built on the bounty of the sea alone, the salmon, eulachon and herring that brought life to the First Nations of the Pacific Northwest.

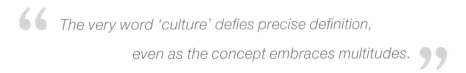

The very word 'culture' defies precise definition, even as the concept embraces multitudes.

During the Neolithic revolution some 10,000 years ago, humans began to domesticate plants and animals. Pastoral nomads settled the marginal reaches of the planet: the sands of the Sahara, the Tibetan plateau and the windswept expanses of the Asian steppe. Agriculturalists took a handful of grasses — wheat, barley, rice, oats, millet and maize — and from their bounty generated surpluses. Food that could be stored allowed for hierarchy, specialization and sedentary life—hallmarks of civilization, as traditionally defined. Great cities arose and, in time, kingdoms, empires and nation-states.

No exhibition can do justice to the full wonder of human cultural experience. The very word "culture" defies precise definition, even as the concept embraces multitudes. An isolated society of a few hundred men and women in the mountains of New Guinea has its own culture, but so do countries such as Ireland and France. Distinct cultures may share similar spiritual beliefs—indeed, this is the norm in lands inspired by Judaism, Christianity, Islam and Buddhism. While language tends to delineate unique worldviews, peoples in Alaska, for example, who have lost the ability to speak in their native tongues, maintain a vibrant sense of culture.

Perhaps the closest we can come to a meaningful definition of culture is to acknowledge each one as a unique and ever-changing constellation identified by its language, religion, social and economic organization, decorative arts, stories, myths, ritual practices and beliefs. The full measure of a culture embraces the actions of its people and the quality of their aspirations, the nature of the metaphors that propel their lives. And no description of a people can be complete without reference to the character of its homeland. Just as landscape defines character, culture springs from a spirit of place.

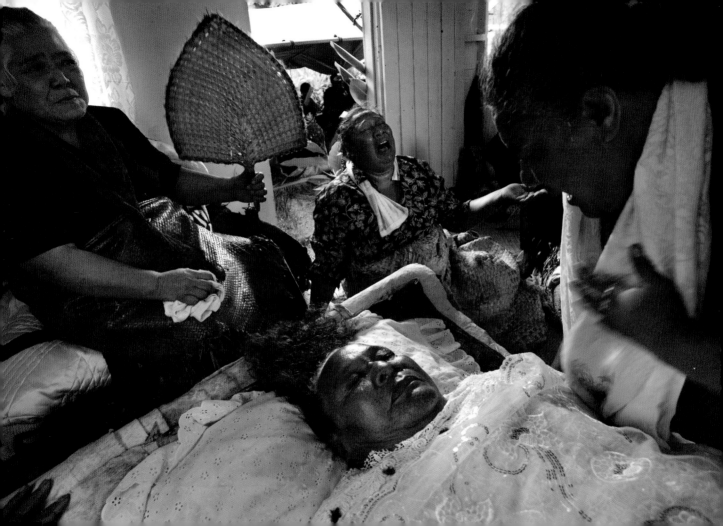

*For all peoples, death has
been the ultimate mystery,
the edge beyond which
life as we know it ends
and wonder begins.*

*Who were these
people who walked
out of Africa* so many
thousands of years ago? If we can
track their subsequent journey
through inherited genetic markers,
it should be possible to find a people
who never left Africa and whose
DNA therefore lacks all evidence of
the mutations that occurred among
our ancestors throughout the
world. Such a people has indeed
been identified, and they have fascinated
anthropologists for decades.

our shared origins

Living today in the searing sands of the Kalahari, 55,000 strong scattered across Botswana, Namibia and southern Angola, the San have long been considered the descendants of a people who once inhabited the entire subcontinent and much of East Africa. Displaced by agriculturalists and pastoral herders, they survived as nomadic hunters and gatherers whose knowledge allowed them to survive in one of the most forbidding desert landscapes on earth. Their extraordinary body of adaptive information is encoded in a native tongue that is a linguistic marvel, totally unrelated to any other known family of languages. In everyday

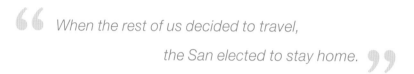

When the rest of us decided to travel,

the San elected to stay home.

English we use 31 sounds. The language of the San has 141, a cacophony of cadence and clicks that many linguists believe echoes the birth of language. Genetic data suggests that this may be the case. The absence of key markers indicates that the San were the first people in the family tree of humanity. If the Irish and the Lakota, the Hawaiian and the Maya are the branches and limbs, the San are the trunk, and quite possibly the oldest culture in the world. When the rest of us decided to travel, the San elected to stay home.

Photo: © Chris Johns/National Geographic Stock

Until the early twentieth century, the San followed the rhythm of their natural world, as they had for perhaps 10,000 years. There was little choice. Their survival depended on their ability to anticipate every nuance of the seasons, every movement of the animals, the growth cycle of every plant. In the Kalahari, water was the constant challenge. For ten months of the year there was none, save what was to be found in the hollows of trees, sucked from beneath the mud with hollow reeds or cached in ostrich eggs. For most of the year the only source of water is liquid found in roots or squeezed from the guts of animals. The San think of themselves as hunters, but they survive by eating plants, as much as twelve pounds of wild melon a day.

Though plants compose the bulk of the San diet, meat is the most desired food because it is the hunt that transforms a boy into a man. Men range across the desert in small hunting parties, walking as far as 50 miles in a day, returning to the fire and their families each night. Hunting in teams, the San watch for signs. Nothing escapes their notice: a bend in a blade of grass; the direction of the tug that snapped a twig; the depth, shape, and condition of a track. Everything is written in the sand. Adultery among the San is a challenge because every human footprint is recognizable. From a single animal track, San hunters can discern direction, time and rate of travel. Antelope are literally run to ground, often over a period of days.

Adultery among the San is a challenge because every human footprint is recognizable.

The hunt is the metaphor that leads into the very heart of San life. A man who does not hunt remains a child. To marry, a man must bring meat to the parents of the bride. A first antelope kill is the high point of youth, a moment recorded in the skin of the hunter by his father, who makes a shallow incision with bone, and rubs into the wound a compound of meat and fat, scarring the right side of the body if the kill is a buck, the left if a doe. The tattoo marks the boy with the heart of a hunter — a potent source of magic, for the San do not simply kill game.

They engage in a dance with the prey, a ritual exchange that ends with the creature making of itself an offering, a sacrifice. Every hunt ends in exhaustion, as the antelope realizes that it cannot escape the pursuit of man. It then stops and turns, and the arrow flies.

 In everyday English we use 31 sounds.

The language of the San has 141.

the genetic story

We are the result of more than a billion years of evolutionary transformation, *and it's encoded in our DNA. If the DNA in any human body were stretched out in a single line it would reach not just to the moon, but to 3,000 celestial spheres equidistant from the earth. In life, this chain is broken and bundled into forty-six chromosomes. In each cell's nucleus, the Y chromosome, which determines male gender, passes from father to son. In each cell's mitochondrion, its energy-producing center, DNA passes from mother to daughter. These two threads of DNA act as a sort of time machine, opening a window on the past.*

About 99.9 percent of human DNA does not vary from person to person. But differences in the remaining 0.1 percent offer vital clues to human ancestry. As genetic information travels through generations, small mutations occur. They are markers that allow population geneticists to reconstruct the story of human origins and migration with a precision that would have been unimaginable a generation ago. By studying individual differences in DNA, lineages of descent can be determined, and the entire journey of humanity can be brought into remarkably precise focus.

ancient wisdom

One of the intense pleasures of travel is the opportunity to live among peoples who have not forgotten the old ways. Just to know that, in the Amazon, Jaguar shaman still journey beyond the Milky Way, that the myths of the Inuit elders still resonate with meaning, that the Buddhists in Tibet still pursue the breath of the Dharma is to remember the central revelation of

Every culture has something to teach the world.

Each is an inspired expression of our collective genius.

anthropology: the idea that the social world in which we live does not exist in some absolute sense, but rather is simply one model of reality, the consequence of one set of intellectual and spiritual choices that our particular cultural lineage made, however successfully, many generations ago. But whether we travel with the nomadic Penan in the forests of Borneo, a Vodoun acolyte in Haiti, or a Maasai warrior on the grasslands of the Serengeti, we learn that there are other options, other possibilities, other ways of thinking and interacting with the earth. Every culture has something to teach the world. Each is an inspired expression of our collective genius.

Consider the greatest cultural sphere ever brought into being by the human imagination, Polynesia, an eighth of the surface of the planet with tens of thousands of islands flung like jewels upon the southern seas. Even today Polynesian sailors can name 250 stars in the night sky. Their navigators can identify atolls beyond the visible horizon by watching the

reverberation of waves across the hull of a canoe. They know that every Pacific island group has its own refractive pattern, read as easily as a forensic scientist reads a fingerprint. Sitting alone in the darkness, they can sense as many as five distinct swells moving through the vessel at any given time, distinguishing those caused by local weather disturbances from the deep currents that pulsate across the ocean and can be followed as readily as a terrestrial explorer would follow a river to the sea. Indeed, if you took all the genius that allowed us to put a man on the moon and applied it to an understanding of the ocean, what you would get is Polynesia.

The ancient city of Timbuktu, located just north of the great bend of the Niger River, was for centuries a thriving port on the sea of sand that is the Western Sahara. When Paris and London were small medieval towns, it was a center of Islamic culture with 150 schools and universities, and some 25,000 students studying astronomy, mathematics, medicine, botany,

 A thirst for seeking is awakened in the endless ocean of sand. The desert hones devotion.

philosophy and religion. Knowledge acquired by ancient Greeks survived to inspire the Renaissance because it had been preserved by great Islamic scholars such as Avicenna, whose writings informed St. Thomas of the philosophy of Aristotle. Until the discovery of the New World, two-thirds of Europe's gold came from Africa. Out of the desert came great slabs of salt, imbued with magical healing properties so valued that salt traded ounce for ounce with the gold of Ghana. Until an Arab boy endured the thirst and privation of a desert crossing, he could not marry or be considered a man. "In the endless ocean of sand," a

sage once said, "the young man realizes that he is but a particle in the universe. Thus is awakened a thirst for seeking. The desert hones his devotion."

> " *The Sahara has a science known to those who have crossed it for centuries.* "

In the Northwest Amazon of Colombia live the People of the Anaconda, the Barasana and Makuna, who believe that their ancestors came up the Milk River from the east in the belly of the sacred serpent. There is no word for time in their languages, yet they have a complex understanding of astronomy, solar calendars, hierarchy and specialization. Their systems of exchange facilitate peace, not war. To marry one must seek a spouse who speaks a different language. Status accrues not to the warrior, but to the man of wisdom.

The Amazon was an artery of civilization, home to millions of human beings.

Their wealth is vested in ritual regalia as elegant as that of a medieval court. Their longhouses, or malocas, rival the great architectural creations of humanity. Their struggle to bring order to the universe, to maintain the energetic flows of life, and the specificity of their beliefs and adaptations, their rules and restrictions, amount essentially to a complex land management plan dictating precisely how human beings in great numbers can thrive in the upland forests of the Amazon. Indeed, it is now recognized that these remarkable peoples are direct descendants of the lost civilizations of the Amazon. They echo the ancient pre-Columbian

past and point a way forward, embodying a model of how human societies can thrive in the Amazon basin without laying waste to the forests.

" *A corona of oropendola feathers really is the sun, each yellow plume a ray.* "

sacred geography

The universe, René Descartes declared in the 17th century, was composed only of "mind and mechanism." With a single phrase, all sentient creatures except humans were devitalized, as was the earth itself. "Science," as Saul Bellow wrote, "made a housecleaning of belief." The triumph of secular materialism became the conceit of modernity. The notion that land could have anima, that the flight of a hawk might have meaning, that beliefs of the spirit could have true resonance, was dismissed as ridiculous.

Most traditional societies would disagree. This is not to say that they view the natural world through a lens of ecological purity. Life in the malarial swamps of New Guinea, the chill winds of Tibet, the white heat of the Sahara, leaves little room for sentiment. What these cultures have done, however, is to forge a traditional mystique of the earth based not only on deep attachment to the land but also on a far more subtle intuition - the idea that the land itself is breathed into being by human consciousness. Mountains, rivers and forests are not perceived as inanimate, as mere props on a stage upon which human drama unfolds. For most peoples of the world, the land is alive, a dynamic force to be embraced and transformed by the human imagination. The result is a profound sense of belonging and connection. A child raised to believe that a mountain is a deity will have a relationship with the natural world very different from that of a youth brought up to believe a mountain is an inert mass of rock ready to be mined.

> *Just as landscape defines character,*
>
> *culture springs from a spirit of place.*

The Indians of the Sierra Nevada de Santa Marta were never fully vanquished by the Spaniards. Descendants of the ancient Tairona civilization — the Arhuacos, Kogi and Wiwa — escaped death and pestilence to settle in a mountain paradise that soars 20,000 feet above the Caribbean coastal plain of Colombia. To this day they remain true to the moral, ecological and spiritual dictates of the Great Mother who spun the world into existence. They are still led and inspired by a ritual priesthood of mamos whose acolytes are taken from their families as infants and sequestered in the kan'kurua, the men's temple, or its immediate environs for 18 years — two nine-year periods that recall the nine months of gestation. They are in the womb of the Great Mother, where they are taught rituals and prayers thought to maintain the cosmic and ecological balance of the earth.

When an initiate is ready, he is led into the light of dawn to see the world as it really is, in all its transcendent beauty. He then sets off on a sacred pilgrimage from the mountains to the sea, and back to the ice and snow at the heart of the world. With him are spiritual teachers, the mamos, who remind him that everything he sees is his to protect.

Dreamtime is a parallel universe where past, future and present merge into one.

When our deep ancestral relatives reached Australia, they went walking and eventually established a matrix of 10,000 clan territories on the most arid of continents. Linking these homelands was a common idea, the Dreaming. It refers to the first dawning, when the Rainbow Serpent and all the ancestral beings created the world, and is remembered in Songlines, the trajectories travelled by the ancestors as they sang the world into being. The Dreaming is what happened at the time of creation, but also what happens now and in eternity.

In the Aboriginal universe there is no past, present or future. Not one of their 670 languages and dialects has a word for time. The obligation of men and women is not to improve upon nature, but to engage in ritual and ceremonial activities considered essential to maintain the world precisely as it was at the moment of creation. Had humanity as a whole followed the ways of the Aborigines, we would not have put a man on the moon, but neither would we be contemplating the consequences of industrial processes that threaten the life supports of the planet.

beauty

If the skin of the average body were laid flat as a map, it would spread over twenty square feet. Had Leonardo da Vinci chosen the human form as his canvas, he could have worked on a surface four times the size of the *Mona Lisa*. For most cultures the body has always been a sensual topography upon which to display their values and celebrate all that is beautiful in their lives.

Decoration began with pigments extracted from the ground in Africa and with vegetable dyes in the Americas, progressing to the indelible mark of the tattoo and the permanent transformation implied by scarification. To be painted or marked was to express solidarity with something greater than self, for the motifs and designs had deep connotations that could only be understood and recognized by those born to the particular cultural reality celebrated by the forms.

 Mentawai devote their lives to the pursuit of aesthetic beauty, approaching every task fully adorned.

In the upper Amazon, among the Shipibo, the delicate lines of purple and black that adorn the shaman's face allow him to dissolve into spirit, becoming a bird of prey, a jaguar or an anaconda. In Borneo, the Kenyan endure four years of intense ritual pain to complete tattoos that are believed to serve as torches to guide the deceased to the next world. The Haida employ ivory needles to inscribe heraldic designs and family totems onto the breast and

between the shoulders, branding the individual with the markings of clan, lineage and family name. Among the Nuba of the Sudan, body art reveals the identity and age of a woman, linking her to a particular cohort with whom she will share the passages of life. In Polynesia, tattooing was the essential rite of passage. Unmarked, a boy could not marry, speak in the presence of elders or engage in anything but the most menial of work. In Samoa it is said that properly executed designs glow in death and creation with an intensity not seen in life, thus revealing the promise of a spirit world everlasting.

Photo: © Carol Beckwith & Angela Fisher

Off the shore of Sumatra on the island of Siberut, the Mentawai people recognize that spirits enliven everything that exists — birds, plants, clouds, even the rainbows that arch across the sky.

> *The human body is a canvas four times the size of the Mona Lisa.*

Rejoicing in the beauty of the world, these divine entities cannot possibly be expected to reside in a human body that is not beautiful. The Mentawai believe that if nature loses its luster, if the landscape becomes drab, if they themselves cease to honor the essence of beauty in

Photo: © Angela Fisher & Carol Beckwith

Photo: © Richard Evans Schultes

their physical presence, the primordial forces of creation will abandon this realm for the settlements of the dead and all life will perish. To respect the ancestors and celebrate the living, Mentawai men and women devote their lives to the pursuit of aesthetic beauty, preening their bodies, filing their teeth, adding brilliant feathers to their hair and inscribing delicate spiral patterns on their bodies. In daily life they approach every task, however mundane, fully adorned. For the Wodaabe, pastoral nomads of the African sands, male beauty is among the most masculine of attributes. Once each year when the desert blooms, they gather for the Geerewol festival where hundreds of young men compete to appear the most beautiful and, better yet, the most charming. The essential and most desirable quality of a man in Wodaabe society is grace and elegance in all things. Fastidious in their finery, with skin lightened by yellow powder and lips and eyes darkened with black kohl, and with their spirits enlivened by love medicines, they dance before a great assembly of unmarried girls who take their measure and ultimately judge which has the greatest togu, or charm. A wink from a boy, a demure glance from a maiden, followed by a slight twitch of the mouth of the dancer indicating where they should meet, and a marriage is made.

ritual & passages

Every culture has rituals that acknowledge essential passages of life —
birth, puberty, marriage and death. Individuals pause from daily routines to
honor significant moments in their existence as a people. It is only natural to
celebrate bountiful harvests, take note of the longest and shortest days of the
year and place a protective cloak of ritual around children as they abandon

innocence for a life of duty, honor and responsibilities. Marking such passages is how we as a conscious species create order and meaning in a universe that may have none.

 White people go to church and speak about god;

we dance in the temple and become god.

Beneath even the most esoteric and baroque rituals, there is almost always an element of the mundane, a practical purpose that facilitates the functioning of the society. The ease with which Wodaabe men and women pursue their romantic impulses, for example, is but one facet of a complex balance of power between the genders. The Wodaabe recognize two forms of marriage. As a child, a boy is betrothed to a girl of his lineage. With this arranged, or kobgal, marriage come a generous dowry and children who will carry on the bloodline. Should a man fall for a woman from another lineage, a frequent occurrence at the Geerewol festival, she is free to elope and marry. As a teegal wife, she will join the household of her new husband.

Photo: © Angela Fisher & Carol Beckwith

Photo: © Carol Beckwith & Angela Fisher

But she does so at a cost. Her dowry is forfeited, and her children remain with their blood father to be raised in his lineage. As a love wife, she is not likely to be welcomed by the kobgal wife of her spouse. From a material point of view it makes little sense to elope, but what matters to the Wodaabe is not wealth and security, but love and relationships. Confronted by the age old challenge of spontaneous passion in conflict with the stability of marriage, the Wodaabe solve the problem by having two kinds of marriage, sensible kobgal partnerships and teegal matches that give release to whimsy, seduction and romance.

In the Kaisut desert of northern Kenya, drought is a regular feature of climate.

Photo: © Carol Beckwith & Angela Fisher

Photo: © Carol Beckwith & Angela Fisher   85

Photo: © Angela Fisher & Carol Beckwith

Photo: © Carol Beckwith & Angela Fisher

Surviving drought is the key adaptive imperative of all pastoral nomads, tribal peoples such as the Rendille, Samburu and Gabra. To guarantee the continuity of the clan, it is vital to maintain herds of camels and cattle large enough for some animals to survive extreme hardships and provide enough capital to rebuild the wealth of the family. To a great extent this liability and obligation determines the structure of the society. To maintain large herds it is useful for a patriarch to have a large number of children, so the societies are typically polygamous. But with men taking multiple wives, virile young men

All photos: © Chris Rainier

may not have partners to marry. The elders solve this problem by dispatching the young men for a period of ten years to remote encampments where they protect the herds from enemy raiders. To make the separation desirable, it is enveloped in prestige. The greatest event of a young man's life is his public circumcision, when he enters the privileged world of the warrior. The ceremony is held once every fourteen years, and those who endure it together are bonded for life.

 *To marry, a Barasana must seek a spouse who speaks a different language.*

Should a lad flinch or cry out as nine slits are made in his foreskin, he will shame his clan for the rest of his life. Few fail, for the honor is immense. Transformed physically, socially and spiritually, the warriors move to the desert, where they live together on a diet of herbs gathered in the shade of frail acacia trees, mixed with milk and blood drawn each night from the jugular of a heifer. To resolve the dilemma of human libido, the warriors are allowed to return periodically to the community and approach unmarried maidens. Pre-marital sexual liaisons are open and tolerated, up until the moment a young woman is betrothed to an elder. The warrior is expected to attend the wedding of his former lover and publicly mock the virility of the old man who has taken his place. A single adaptive challenge, surviving drought, reverberates through the entire culture, defining for these nomadic tribes what it means to be human.

Photo: © Chris Rainier

quest for spirit

The pursuit of spiritual accomplishment has always been entwined with the ultimate mystery of death. The primordial spiritual impulse was born of the hunt and our Paleolithic ancestors' need to rationalize the terrible fact that to live they had to kill the thing they loved most, the animals they hunted. Shamanism addressed this dilemma by empowering certain rare individuals to mediate directly with animal spirits and all the forces of nature. To this day, from Mongolia to the Amazon, the high Arctic to the forests of Siberia, shamans invoke techniques of ecstasy to access distant metaphysical realms where they alone can work their deeds of medical, mystical and spiritual rescue. The shaman, as Joseph Campbell wrote, swims in the mystic waters the rest of us would drown in. He or she chooses to enter spiritual dimensions that most people do not want to imagine.

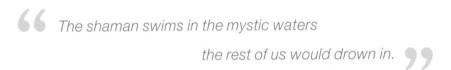

The shaman swims in the mystic waters

the rest of us would drown in.

Among the Barasana, the shaman's most prized possession is a six-inch crystal of quartz, worn around the neck with a single strand of palm fiber. It is both the penis and the crystallized semen of Father Sun, and within it are thirty colors, all distinct energies that must be balanced in sacred ritual. The necklace is also the shaman's house, the place he enters

when he ingests yagé, the hallucinogenic potion also known as ayahuasca. Once inside the crystal, the shaman looks out at the world, watching the ways of the animals, harnessing and restoring the energy of all creation.

With the Neolithic revolution, the poetry of the shaman was displaced by the prose of the priesthood. If the role of the shaman was to facilitate the release of the individual's spirit and wild genius, providing direct access to the divine, the goal of the priest was to draw the individual into the comfort and constraints of an established religious ideology, often in the service of the state. And so were born the great religions: Judaism, Christianity, Islam, Hinduism and

Photo: © Thomas L. Kelly

Buddhism. The essence of Buddhism is distilled in the Four Noble Truths. All life is suffering. The cause of suffering is ignorance, which is not stupidity but the tendency of human beings to cling to their own centrality in the stream of divine existence.

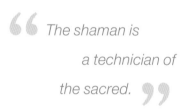 *The shaman is a technician of the sacred.*

Ignorance itself can be overcome by embracing contemplative practice, the fourth of the postulates, which

Photo: © Chris Rainier

promises spiritual transformation on a path informed by 2,500 years of empirical observation and study of the nature of the mind. A Buddhist lama once remarked that in Tibet people do not believe that Americans went to the moon, but they did. Americans may not believe, he added, that Tibetan Buddhists can achieve enlightenment in one lifetime, but they can.

The one constant in our quest for the spirit is a universal desire to look beyond the chasm of death and achieve transformation, illumination and insight. This impulse is so prevalent that it must be seen as a fundamental human need. How we slake this spiritual thirst is simply a matter of choice and cultural inclination.

Photo: © Steve McCurry/Magnum Photos

Among the Lakota, mystic illumination comes through the pain of ordeal, as the warrior hangs by hooks driven through his flesh and attached by rope to the Sun Dance pole, the axis mundi of creation. In Sufi tradition, acolytes spin their spirits into trance.

In West Africa, spirit possession is the hand of divine grace. The living give birth to the dead; the ancestors become the spirits. As the people honor the gods, the spirits must serve the living, returning in sacred ritual to momentarily displace the soul of the believer, so that human being and god become one and the same. As the Haitians say, "White people go to church and speak about god; we dance in the temple and become god."

If there is one certainty in our spiritual quest, it is that no culture has a monopoly on the route to the divine. Those who believe they do are wrong and dangerous.

66 No culture has a monopoly

on the route to the divine. 99

endangered

Even among those sympathetic to the plight of indigenous peoples, there is a sense that these cultures, quaint and colorful though they may be, are somehow destined to fade away, as if by natural law, unfortunate victims of the unrelenting pace of the modern world. Nothing could be further from the truth. In every case these are dynamic living peoples being driven out of existence by identifiable and overwhelming external forces. This is actually an optimistic observation, for it suggests that if human beings are the agents of cultural destruction, we can be the facilitators of cultural survival.

Every language is an old growth forest of the mind.

In 1871 buffalo outnumbered people in North America. Within nine years the buffalo were gone, systematically slaughtered as part of a deliberate government policy to destroy the Lakota Sioux and all the great cultures of the Plains. Philip Sheridan, who orchestrated the campaign, encouraged the U.S. Congress to mint a commemorative medal with a dead buffalo on one side and a discouraged Native American on the other. In 1879 Argentina launched a military campaign with the expressed goal of exterminating the native population of the Pampa. The people of Tasmania were annihilated within 75 years of contact. As recently as 1902 the Australian parliament formally debated whether or not Aborigines were human beings.

Photo: © Wade Davis

Photo: © David Hiser

Photo: © Wade Davis

These terrible events happened not in the distant past but in the lifetimes of our own grandparents, and they continue to this day.

Genocide, the physical extermination of a people, is universally condemned. Ethnocide, the destruction of a people's way of life, is in many quarters sanctioned and endorsed as appropriate development policy. Modernity provides the rationale for disenfranchisement, with the real goal too often being the extraction of natural resources on an industrial scale from territories occupied for generations by indigenous peoples whose ongoing presence on the land proves to be an inconvenience.

Such has been the fate of the Penan, the last nomads of the Borneo rainforest, whose homeland for two generations has been ravaged by the highest rate of industrial deforestation in the world. For the Malaysian government, the existence of tribal society living freely in the forest was an embarrassment, and it set in place programs intended to emancipate the Penan from their backwardness, which meant freeing them from who they were as a people. When the Penan resisted, blockading the logging roads with rattan barricades, blowpipes

Photo: © Richard Evans Schultes

against bulldozers, they were said to be standing in the way of development, which became grounds for dispossessing them and destroying their way of life. Their disappearance was then said to be inevitable, as such archaic folk cannot be expected to survive in the twenty-first century.

Every fortnight an elder carries into the grave the last syllables of an ancient tongue.

A native elder once said that there are only three questions in life; Who am I? Where do I come from? Where am I going? The clash of cultures in the wake of European settlement, he suggested,

All photos this page: © Mauricio Lima

RIO +20
DILMA
COM QUE CARA
VOCÊ CHEGA?

Photo: © Caroline Bennett

was devastating for native people not only because of the terrible impact of diseases and the violence of frontier wars, but also because the dominance and religious certainty of the newcomers allowed them to tell indigenous peoples of every nation that their answers to these fundamental questions were wrong and had been wrong for all of their histories.

 If humans are the agents of cultural destruction,

we can be the facilitators of cultural survival.

Power gave credence to dogma, just as it did in the case of the Chinese government's conquest of Tibet. Reducing the infinite permutations of culture and consciousness to a simple opposition of owners and workers, capitalist and proletariat, Marxism—formulated by a German philosopher in the Reading Room of the British Library—was in a sense the perfect triumph of the mechanistic view of existence inspired by Descartes. Society itself was a machine that could be engineered for the betterment of all. The attempt of revolutionary cadre in scores of nations to impose Marxist thought, a European idea, on peoples as diverse as the

Photo: © Carol Beckwith & Angela Fisher

Photo: © Brent Stirton/Getty Images

Photo: © Brent Stirton/Getty Images

All photos: © Hamid Sardar-Afkhami

Nenets reindeer herders of Siberia, the Dogon living beneath the burial caves of their ancestors in the cliffs of Mali, the Laotians and Vietnamese, the Bantu, Bambara and Fulani would appear almost laughably naive had not the consequences proved so disastrous for so much of humanity. When Mao Zedong famously whispered into the ear of a young Dalai Lama that all religion was poison, the Tibetan spiritual leader knew what was coming. The Chinese government launched a total assault on every facet of Tibetan civilization. Over a million Tibetans died as 6,000 monasteries, temples and religious shrines were reduced to rubble, blasted from the air and ground by artillery and bombs. It is neither change nor technology that threatens the integrity of culture. It is power, the crude force of domination and violence.

All photos: © Lynn Johnson

All photos this page: © Lynn Johnson

Photo: © Lynn Johnson

Photo: © Steve McCurry/Magnum Photos

language loss

Just as we have come to recognize that every culture has something to contribute at the council of human wisdom, the very voices of humanity are being silenced. Of the 7,000 languages spoken today, fully half are not being passed on to children. On average, every fortnight an elder dies and carries into the grave the last syllables of an ancient tongue. What this means is that within a single generation or two we will be witnessing the loss of fully half of humanity's social, cultural and intellectual legacy.

A language is not merely a set of grammatical rules or a vocabulary. It is a flash of the human spirit, the vehicle by which the soul of a culture comes into the material world. Every language is an old growth forest of the mind, a watershed of thought, an ecosystem of spiritual possibilities.

All photos: © Lynn Johnson

globalization

Just before she died, anthropologist Margaret Mead spoke of her concern that, as we drift toward a more homogenous world, we are laying the foundations of a blandly amorphous, generic modern culture that will have no rivals. The entire imagination of humanity might be confined, she feared, to a single intellectual and spiritual modality. Her nightmare was the possibility that we might wake one day and not even remember what had been lost. Our species has been around for some 200,000 years. The Neolithic Revolution, which gave us agriculture, occurred only 10,000 years ago. Modern industrial society is scarcely 300 years old. This shallow history should not suggest that we have all the answers for all the challenges that will confront us in the coming millennia.

 *The triumph of secular materialism*

became the conceit of modernity.

All cultures are ethnocentric, fiercely loyal to their own interpretations of reality. Indeed, the names of many indigenous societies translate as "the people," implying that every other human is a savage. We, too, are culturally myopic, often forgetting that modernity is but an expression of our cultural values. It is not some objective force removed from the con-straints of culture. And it is certainly not the true and only pulse of history. It is merely a

Photo: © Steve McCurry/Magnum Photos

constellation of beliefs, convictions and economic paradigms that represent one way of doing things.

Our achievements have been stunning. The development within the last century of a modern, scientific system of medicine alone represents one of the greatest episodes in human endeavor. Sever a limb in a car accident, and you won't want to be taken to an herbalist. But these accomplishments do not make the Western paradigm exceptional or suggest that it ought to monopolize the path to the future.

An anthropologist from a distant planet landing in the United States would see many wondrous things. But he, she or it would also encounter a culture that reveres marriage, yet allows half of its marriages to end in divorce; admires its elderly, yet has grandparents living with grandchildren in only 6 percent of its households; loves its children, yet embraces a "24/7" slogan that promotes total devotion to the workplace at the expense of family. By the age of 18, the average American youth has spent three years watching television or playing video games. One in five adults is clinically obese. The nation consumes two-thirds of the

Photo: © A Yin

world's production of antidepressant drugs, even as it spends more money on armaments and war than the collective military budgets of its seventeen closest rivals. Technological wizardry is balanced by an economic model of production and consumption that challenges the very life support systems of the planet. Our way of life, inspired in so many ways, is not the paragon of humanity's potential.

When we project modernity as the inevitable destiny of all human societies, we are being disingenuous in the extreme. The Western model of development has been based on the false promise that people who follow its dictates will achieve the material prosperity enjoyed by a handful of nations of the West. In reality, development often implies a process by which the individual is torn from his past, propelled into an uncertain future, only to secure a place on the bottom rung of an economic ladder that goes nowhere. The fate of the vast majority of

 Our way of life, inspired in so many ways,

is not the paragon of humanity's potential.

All photos: © A Yin

those who sever their ties with their traditions will not be to attain the prosperity of the West, but to join the legions of urban poor, trapped in squalor, struggling to survive.

Globalization, capital in pursuit of cheap labor, is celebrated with iconic intensity. But what are the real consequences? In Bangladesh, garment workers are paid pennies to sew clothing that retails in the United States and Canada for tens of dollars. Eighty percent of the toys and sporting goods sold in America are produced in sweatshops in China, where millions work for wages as low as 12 cents an hour, 400,000 die prematurely each year due to air pollution, and 400 million people do not have access to potable water. Outside major industrial nations, globalization has not brought integration and harmony, but a firestorm of change that has swept away languages and cultures, ancient skills and visionary wisdom.

151

joy of culture

People sometimes ask why it would matter to those living in, say, Los Angeles if some culture in Africa were extinguished through assimilation or violence. Perhaps it wouldn't, any more than the disappearance of Los Angeles would matter to that distant tribe. But it could be argued that the loss of either way of life does matter to humanity as a whole. It is a basic issue of human rights.

Who is to say that the American perspective on reality matters more than that of the Tuareg? At a more fundamental level, we have to ask ourselves: What kind of world do we want to live in? Most Americans will never encounter a camel caravan of blue-robed Tuareg moving slowly across an ocean of white sand. Many people will never see a painting by Monet or hear a Mozart symphony. But does this mean that the world would not be a lesser place without these artists and cultures and their unique interpretations of reality?

 Culture alone allows us to reach for the better angels of our nature.

If there is one lesson of anthropology, it is that culture is not trivial. It is not decoration or artifice, the songs we sing or even the prayers we chant. Culture is a blanket of comfort that gives meaning to lives. It is a body of knowledge that allows the individual to make sense out of the infinite sensations of consciousness, to find meaning and order in a universe that

ultimately has neither. Most essentially, it is a body of laws and traditions, moral and ethical codes that insulate a people from the barbaric heart that history suggests lies just beneath the surface of all human societies. Culture alone allows us to reach, as Abraham Lincoln said, for the better angels of our nature.

To acknowledge the wonder of other cultures is not to denigrate our way of life, but to recognize with some humility that other peoples, flawed as they too may be, contribute to our collective heritage, the human repertoire of ideas, beliefs and adaptations that have allowed us as a species to thrive. To appreciate this truth is to sense the

Photo: © Timothy Allen

tragedy inherent in the loss of a language or the assimilation of a people. To lose a culture is to lose something of our selves.

This is not to suggest naively that we attempt to mimic the ways of non-industrial societies, or that any culture be asked to forfeit its right to benefit from the wizardry of technology. The goal is not to freeze people in time. Cultures are not museum pieces; they are communities of real people with real needs. The issue is not the traditional versus the modern, but the right of free peoples to choose the components of their lives. The point is not to deny access, but rather to ensure that all peoples are able to benefit from the genius of modernity on their own terms, without that engagement demanding the death of their ethnicity and their identity as a people.

" To lose a culture is to lose something of our selves. "

The cultures celebrated in this exhibition embody "ancient wisdom in a modern world." But this should not suggest that they are vestigial, archaic voices stranded in time, with only a vague advisory role in contemporary life. They are all very much alive and fighting not only for their cultural survival but also to take part in a global dialogue that will define the future of life on earth. Their voices matter because they tell us that there are alternatives, other ways of orienting human beings in social, spiritual and ecological space. They remind us that the path we have taken is not the only one available. They bear witness to the folly of those who say that we cannot change, as we all know we must, the fundamental manner in which we inhabit this planet.

It is within this diversity of knowledge and practice, intuition and interpretation, promise and hope, that we will all rediscover the enchantment of being what we are, a conscious species fully capable of ensuring that all peoples in all gardens find a way to flourish.

photo captions & credits

Front Cover | Randy Olson, OlsonFarlow.com | *Indus River, Mohenjo Daro, Pakistan*
On the Indus river, bird hunters employ a technique that has been practiced for 5,000 years, according to archaeological records. They tie a living heron to a hoop, and then, wearing masks made from bird skins, submerge themselves to their necks in the water. Wiggling their heads to mimic swimming birds, they attract their prey and grab the wild birds as they land on the water.

Page 4-5 | Chris Rainier | *Sahara desert, Niger*
The Tuareg know the desert as a sailor knows the sea. When the wind blows they know what kind of wind. When a cloud gathers they can smell the rain. If thirsty they can sense the scent of water. With the camels there is a trust built on 2,000 years. They know that they can close their eyes, and the camels will lead them home. The Sahara has a science that is known to those who have crossed it for centuries.

Page 10 | Steve McCurry/Magnum Photos | *Lhasa, Tibet*
A Tibetan woman in the Barkhor, the sacred heart of the ancient Tibetan capital of Lhasa. Though recognized as a World Heritage site by the United Nations, much of the Barkhor has been demolished by the Chinese government over the last 15 years. 2000

Page 12, upper left | Brent Stirton/Getty Images | *Loryra, South Omo, Ethiopia*
A woman of the Dassanech people of the Lower Omo Valley in South West Ethiopia. 2007

Page 12, lower left | Amy Toensing | *Ha'apai Islands, Tonga*
Longo Paea Moala gathers pandanus leaves after soaking them in the ocean for days to soften and lighten the color. The leaves are dried in the sun for two to three days and used to weave different types of mats and clothing. Tonga is one of the last surviving monarchies in the Pacific islands. A recent push towards democratic reform has challenged the people of Tonga to maintain their cultural heritage while embracing change, the one constant in human history. 2007

Page 13 | Steve McCurry/Magnum Photos | *Rajasthan, India*
Hindu villagers participate in the Holi Festival in Rajasthan. 1996

Page 14 | Randy Olson, OlsonFarlow.com | *Indus River, Mohenjo Daro, Pakistan*
See caption for front cover.

Page 15 | Steve McCurry/Magnum Photos | *Henan Province, China*
Young monks train at the Shaolin Monastery in Henan Province, China. The physical strength and dexterity displayed by the monks is remarkable, as is their serenity. At its core Buddhism is simply a wisdom philosophy, a set of contemplative practices, a spiritual path informed by 2,500 years of empirical observation and deduction that, if followed, offers the certain promise of a transformation of the human heart. 2004

Page 16, upper left | Steve McCurry/Magnum Photos | *Kyaiktiyo, Myanmar*
Burnished with prayers, the Golden Rock is the destination of countless pilgrims because it is one of the most important of Buddhist shrines in Southeast Asia. Legend has it that the rock is kept balanced in place by a single strand of hair from the Buddha's head. 1994

Page 16, right | Angela Fisher & Carol Beckwith | *South Sudan*
A Dinka boy from South Sudan lavishes endless care and affection on his animals, which he considers part of his family. He is named after his favored ox, his Namesake Ox, in the hope he will mature with the same strength and beauty. He and his Namesake Ox are as one. As he grows up, the animal will accompany him everywhere, even as he courts a potential lover by singing songs that extol both her beauty and that of the magnificent animal at his side. 2006

Page 16, lower left | Angela Fisher & Carol Beckwith | *Niger*
While Wodaabe men flaunt their beauty in the Yaake charm dance, each attempting to appear the most beguiling, an elder woman in a yellow veil offers both praise and mockery. If a man's performance is exceptional, she dashes toward

him yelling "yeee hooo!" and gently butts him with her head on his torso. If she is displeased with his efforts, she points a bird beak at him, automatically disqualifying him for not being beautiful and charming enough. She is generously paid off in cattle before the dance begins so has rarely disqualified anyone. 1990

Page 18 | Timothy Allen | *Central highlands of Papua New Guinea*
A man and woman share an intimate moment during a courtship ritual in the central highlands of Papua New Guinea.

Page 21 | Angela Fisher & Carol Beckwith | *Namibia*
A Himba family—father, mother, children and dogs—stands before their home, a small temporary dwelling constructed of branches packed with plaster made from cattle dung and clay. Cattle hides provide sleeping mats, as well as material for the skirts worn by women and children. Calabashes, or gourds, hold the milk that is the mainstay of the Himba diet. Totally dependent on their herds, the Himba were traditionally considered to be the greatest cattle breeders of Africa. 1994

Page 22 | Hamid Sardar-Afkhami | *Deloun district, Olgii Province, Mongolia*
A Kazakh woman pacifies her two grandchildren while their mother goes out to milk the yaks. 2001

Page 25 | Hamid Sardar-Afkhami | *Sornuk Valley, Hovsgol Province, Outer Mongolia*
A Duhalar child falls asleep on a white reindeer as her mother milks the herd nearby. 2006

Page 26 | Lynn Johnson | *Dimen, China*
Bending to the constant rhythm of farming, a Dong woman gathers rice shoots from a plot near home to sow in terraced fields. Come what may, fire or flood, this is the work that still feeds her family and stands at the heart of her culture. Her language, with 15 distinct tones, is considered one of the most difficult in the world to master. The Dong are one of 55 major ethnic groups in China, 100 million people altogether, dominated by the Han, who number 1.2 billion worldwide, fully a sixth of the global population.

Page 28 | Amy Toensing | *Ha'apai Islands, Tonga*
Tongan women mourn the passing of Kalisi Lolohea Paonga in the village of Pangai, on the island of Ha'apai, Tonga. Cultural rules dictate where family and friends are positioned at a wake. The woman with a fan is Kalisi Lolohea Paonga's beloved Aunty. She is the only one allowed to sit above the body of the deceased. Everyone else has to sit below on the floor. For all peoples, death has been the ultimate mystery, the edge beyond which life as we know it ends and wonder begins. How a culture comes to terms with the inexorable separation that death implies determines, to a great extent, their spiritual beliefs and religious practices. 2007

Page 30 | Chris Johns/National Geographic Stock | *Nyae Nyae Conservancy, Namibia*
For the San, the sun is not a source of life, but a symbol of death. The possibility of dying of thirst is a constant, even in the season of rains. As dry winds sweep over the desert, the spirits of the dead appear as dust devils spinning across a gray and yellow horizon. In good years, the rains bring relative abundance. Pools of water form on the sand. Equipped only with digging sticks, collecting bags, woven nets and ostrich shells to carry water, the people move about in small bands, extended family units that occasionally come together to celebrate a harvest of fruits or seeds, or the presence of game. These wanderings are not random. Each passage traverses known ground, time-honored territories that resonate with narratives, each granting ownership of a particular resource to a band of people. The resource might be a tree or shrub, or a recognized source of honey, the most highly prized of nectars.

Page 32-33 | Chris Johns/National Geographic Stock | *Near Welkom, Kalahari-Gemsbok National Park, Botswana*

The San travel light: short bow and a quiver of arrows made from root bark capped in the scrotum of the prey; fire-making sticks; a hollow reed for sucking water; a knife and short spear; a blob of vegetable gum to make repairs; a sharpened stick for holding meat to flame. The San bows have an effective range of but 27 yards. The arrows rarely penetrate the prey. They nick the skin, but generally that is enough, because the arrows are tipped in deadly toxin derived from the grubs of beetles that feed on the leaves of a desert tree. The sun-dried venom provokes convulsions, paralysis and death.

Page 34 | Brent Stirton/Getty Images | *Kalahari Desert, South Africa*

Abijong Kruiper, 63, is the oldest of his tribe. He often stands on one leg while waiting, resting one leg on the other. If the San associate the sun with death, fire symbolizes life, the unity of the people and the survival of the family. A gift of meat formalizes the betrothal of a woman; divorce is finalized the moment she simply returns to her family's fire. A mother gives birth in the darkness and announces the delivery by moving back into the circle of firelight. When an elder grows too old and weak to continue with the people, he is left behind to die, protected from the hyenas by a circle of thorn scrub and a fire at his feet to light his way into the next world. 2006

Page 37 | Brent Stirton/Getty Images | *Kalahari Desert, Namibia/South Africa*

For the San there are two great spirits: the Great God of the Eastern Sky and the lesser God of the West, a source of negativity and darkness, the custodian of the dead. To ward off the God of the West, to deflect the arrows of disease and misfortune, the San dance around the fire, casting their beings into trance. The vital force of life that resides in the belly rises up the spine as a vapor, touches the base of the skull, diffuses through the body and spins the spirit into a higher consciousness. The healing dance ends with the hunters around the fire, having teased the flames and the gods by placing their own heads in the burning coals. 2006

Page 40 | Randy Olson, OlsonFarlow.com | *Samoa*

The training of the Polynesian wayfinder, or navigator, begins in infancy as he is placed in tidal pools for hours at a time so he might feel and absorb the rhythms of the sea. If, on his first deep ocean voyage, he becomes sick from the swells, his teacher will tie him to a rope and pull him behind the canoe until the nausea passes. It was by such devotion and rigor that the Polynesian ancestors settled the Pacific. 2000

Page 43 | Randy Olson, OlsonFarlow.com | *Ofu Island, Samoa*

Men carrying handmade baskets on a plantation on the island of Ofu. European contact brought chaos and devastation to Samoa. The two pillars of Polynesian society, aside from the navigators, were the chief and the priest. The authority of the chief was based on his capacity to control and distribute surplus food. The power of the priest lay in a spiritual capacity to enforce tapu, the sacred rules of the culture. When European diseases swept through the islands, killing up to 85 percent of the people on the Marquesas in less than a month, the demographic collapse destroyed the traditional economy, even as it compromised the priests, who had no capacity to sanction foreigners who violated tapu with impunity, and by some miracle, were immune to pestilence. Missionaries, who in considerable numbers crossed the beaches in the wake of sustained contact, blamed the people themselves for their misfortunes, even as they dismissed their religious beliefs as crude idolatry. 2000

Page 44, upper left | Wade Davis | *Oahu, Hawaii*

Hokule'a, named after the sacred star of Hawaii, is a replica of the great seafaring canoes of ancient Polynesia. It is a double-hulled open-decked catamaran 62 feet long, 19 feet wide, lashed together by some 5 miles of rope, with a fully loaded displacement of some 24,000 pounds. Launched in 1975, the Hokule'a has crisscrossed the Pacific, visiting nearly every island group of the Polynesian triangle, from Hawaii to New Zealand, and south and east to Rapa Nui, or Easter Island. Not a single modern navigational device is on board. There are only the multiple senses of the navigator, the knowledge of the crew, and the pride, authority and power of an entire people reborn. 2005

Page 44, lower left | Lynn Johnson | *Island of Hawaii, Hawaii*
Steven Hanaloa Helela and his students are training off the island of Hawaii. Traditional Polynesian navigation was based on dead reckoning; Polynesians only knew where they were by remembering precisely how they got there. Over the course of a long ocean voyage, the wayfinder, or navigator, had to remember every shift of wind, speed and current, every sign of the stars, moon and sun without benefit of the written word. It was an impossible challenge for early European sailors, who for the most part hugged the shores of continents until the British solved the problem of longitude with the invention of the chronometer. Yet ten centuries before Christ, the ancestors of these students sailed east into the rising sun, settling every significant island group of the Pacific.

Page 46 | Brent Stirton/Getty Images | *Timbuktu, Mali*
The Sankore Mosque, one of three Islamic monuments in Timbuktu listed by the United Nations as World Heritage sites, is currently threatened by a civil war in Mali. The conflict has pitted the nomadic Tuareg of the north against the Bambara and other tribes that control the reins of power in Bamako, the capital of Mali. 2009

Page 47 | Brent Stirton/Getty Images | *Timbuktu, Mali*
In 1914, when the French took control of Timbuktu, they confiscated the ancient manuscripts, threatened the scholars with jail and taught the children that their ancestors were not Arab or Berber, Tamashek or Tuareg, but Gaul. The library pictured here is one of the oldest in the world. It is filled with ancient manuscripts that have survived throughout the centuries. 2009

Page 48-49 | Chris Rainier | *Sahara desert, Niger*
See caption for page 4-5.

Page 51 | Wade Davis | *Rio Apaporis, Northwest Amazon, Colombia*
The Amazon at the time of European contact was no empty forest, but an artery of civilization and home to millions of human beings. Within generations, diseases such as measles and smallpox, unknown in the New World, swept away 90 percent of the Amerindian population, from Tierra del Fuego to the Arctic. 2009

Page 52 | Wade Davis | *Rio Piraparaná, Northwest Amazon, Colombia*
There is no beginning and end in Barasana thought, no sense of a linear progression of time, destiny or fate. Theirs is a fractal world in which no event has a life of its own, and any number of ideas can coexist in parallel levels of perception and meaning. Every object must be understood at various levels of analysis. A rapid is an impediment to travel but also a house of the ancestors, with both a front and back door. A stool is not a symbol of a mountain; it is in every sense an actual mountain with the shaman sitting at the summit. A row of stools is the ancestral anaconda, and the patterns painted onto the wood of the stools depict both the journey of the ancestors and the striations that decorate the serpent's skin. A corona of oropendola feathers really is the sun, each yellow plume a ray. 2009

Page 53, upper right | Wade Davis | *Rio Piraparaná, Northwest Amazon, Colombia*
Men smoke tobacco during the celebration of Cassava Woman, a 72-hour ritual in which the men consume copious amounts of coca powder, tobacco snuff and yagé, an exceedingly potent psychoactive preparation. When they say that they travel through multiple dimensions during their rituals while under its powerful influence, reliving the journey of the ancestors and alighting on the sacred sites, it is because they really do.

Page 53, lower right | Wade Davis | *Rio Piraparaná, Northwest Amazon, Colombia*
In the beginning, before the creation of seasons, before the Ancestral Mother, Romi Kumu, opened her womb, before her blood and breast milk gave rise to rivers and her ribs to the mountain ridges of the world, there was only chaos in the universe. Spirits and demons known as "He" preyed on their own kindred, bred without thought, committed incest without consequence and devoured their own young. Romi Kumu responded by destroying the world with fire and floods. Then she

turned the inundated and charred world upside down, creating a flat and empty template from which life could emerge once again. As Woman Shaman she then gave birth to a new world: land, water, forest and animals. 2009

Page 54 | Randy Olson, OlsonFarlow.com | *Epulu, Democratic Republic of the Congo*
Pygmy girls paint each other in support of their brothers, who are going through the Kumbi initiation ceremony. 2004

Page 57 | Timothy Allen | *Central African Republic*
The Bayaka go to great lengths to search for wild honey, the most desirable product of their forest homeland. Mongonje, a Bayaka tribesman, scales a tree that soars 130 feet into the canopy of the richest tropical rainforest in West Africa.

Page 58 | Randy Olson, OlsonFarlow.com | *Democratic Republic of the Congo*
Pygmy Boys wear ritual skirts as they go through their Kumbi initiation, the ceremony of circumcision that marks their passage from innocence into experience, from childhood into the life of a hunter. 2004

Page 60 | Wade Davis | *Sierra Nevada de Santa Marta, Colombia*
An Arhuaco family on pilgrimage has gathered around an evening fire. As they travel up and down the mountain slopes, they refer to their movements as threads, laid down over time by a community to form a protective cloak over the Earth. When the women plant a field, they sow lines of crops parallel to the sides of the plot. The men work their way across the field in a horizontal direction. Should the domains of man and woman be superimposed, the result is a fabric. The garden is a piece of cloth. 2008

Page 61, left | Wade Davis | *Sierra Nevada de Santa Marta, Colombia*
Arhuaco men walking through the ruins of an ancient settlement of the Tairona, their direct ancestors. According to myth, the mountains were dreamed into existence when the Great Mother spun her thoughts and conceived the nine layers of the universe. To stabilize the world, she thrust her spindle into its axis and lifted up the massif. Then, uncoiling a length of cotton thread, she delineated the horizons of the civilized world, tracing a circle around the base of the Sierra Nevada, which she declared to be the homeland of her children. This primordial act of creation is never forgotten. The loom, the act of spinning, the notion of a community woven into the fabric of a landscape are vital and living metaphors that consciously guide and direct the lives of the people of the Sierra. 2008

Page 61, right | Wade Davis | *Sierra Nevada de Santa Marta, Colombia*
When the Arhuacos pray they often clasp in their hands small bundles of white cotton, symbols of the Great Mother who taught them to spin. The circular movement of hands in prayer recalls the moment when the Great Mother spun the universe into being. Her commandment was to protect everything she had woven. This was her law. 2008

Page 62 | Wade Davis | *Sierra Nevada de Santa Marta, Colombia*
In the hands of Danilo Villafaña, a political leader of the Arhuacos, is a poporo, a gourd containing lime used to potentiate hayu, or coca, their most sacred plant. The conical hats worn by Arhuaco men represent the snowfields of the sacred peaks. The hairs on a person's body echo the forest trees that cover the mountain flanks. Every element of nature is imbued with higher significance. Even the most modest of creatures can be seen as a teacher, and the smallest grain of sand is a mirror of the universe. 2008

Page 63 | Wade Davis | *Santa Marta, Colombia*
Arhuaco men and women on pilgrimage to the sea where many of their sacred sites have been violated by modern construction. In their cosmic scheme people are vital, for it is only through the human heart and imagination that the Great Mother may become manifest. For the Indians of the Sierra Nevada, people are not the problem but the solution. They call themselves the Elder Brothers and consider their mountains to be the "heart of the world." We outsiders who threaten the earth through our ignorance of the sacred law are dismissed as the

Younger Brothers. Living just two hours by air from Miami Beach, the Elder Brothers stare out to sea from the heights of the Sierra Nevada, praying for our well-being and that of the entire earth. 2009

Page 64 | Wade Davis | *Arnhem Land, Northern Territory, Australia*
Everything on earth is held together by Songlines; everything is subordinate to the Dreaming, which is constant but ever changing. Every landmark is wedded to a memory of its origins, and yet always being born. Every animal and object resonates with the pulse of an ancient event, while still being dreamed into being. The world as it exists is perfect, though constantly in the process of being formed. The land is encoded with everything that has ever been, everything that ever will be, in every dimension of reality. 2008

Page 66, upper left | Wade Davis | *Arnhem Land, Northern Territory, Australia*
Fire is both a tool and a symbol of regeneration and purification. Dreamtime is neither a dream nor a measure of the passage of time. It is the very realm of the ancestors, a parallel universe where the ordinary laws of time, space and motion do not apply, where past, future and present merge into one. It is a place Europeans can only approximate in sleep, and thus it became known to early English settlers as the Dreaming. But the term is misleading. A dream by Western definition is a state of consciousness divorced from the real world. Dreamtime, by contrast, is the real world, or at least one of two realities experienced in the daily lives of the Aborigines. 2008

Page 66, lower left | Wade Davis | *Arnhem Land, Northern Territory, Australia*
To walk the Songlines is to become part of the ongoing creation of the world, a place that both exists and is still being formed. The Aborigines are not merely attached to the earth, they are essential to its existence. Without the land they would die. But without the people, the ongoing process of creation would cease and the earth would wither. Through movement and sacred rituals, the people maintain access to Dreamtime and play a dynamic and ongoing role in the world of the ancestors. 2008

Page 67 | Wade Davis | *Arnhem Land, Northern Territory, Australia*
For over 55,000 years, the Aboriginal peoples of Australia thrived as hunters and gatherers, and guardians of their world. In all that time the desire to improve upon the natural world had never touched them. They accepted life as it was, a cosmological whole, the unchanging creation of the first dawn, when earth and sky separated and the original Ancestor, the Rainbow Serpent, brought into being all the primordial ancestors who through their thoughts, dreams and journeys sang the world into existence. This woman stands in a sacred site of the Rainbow Serpent.

Page 68 | Timothy Allen | *Near Lake Chad, Niger*
Among the Wodaabe, pastoral nomads of the sub-Sahara of Niger, charm and beauty are the most desirable character traits of both men and women. At the annual Geerewol festival, men adorn their faces with exquisite decoration and show their beauty in dances. They are judged by women - like those pictured here - who reveal their grace and elegance in displays of calabashes, or gourds, and the many beautiful objects they place inside them.

Page 71 | Chris Rainier | *Mentawai Islands, Indonesia*
A tattooed man is identified by traditional tattoos from his homeland, the Mentawai Islands, Indonesia.

Page 72 | Carol Beckwith & Angela Fisher | *Kenya*
A Swahili woman from Kenya decorates her hands and feet with designs made from henna, a dye derived from a powdered leaf mixed with water and the juice of unripe lemons. The designs are drawn with a fine twig; five to six applications are required to ensure that the henna doesn't fade too soon, a process that takes up to 12 hours. In modern times, a black synthetic dye is used to enhance the elaborate designs. A Swahili woman who appears in public must remain concealed in black veils and long robes. Her hands and feet are the only parts of her body that may be seen. 2006

Page 73 | Angela Fisher & Carol Beckwith | *Kenya*
A Turkana bride from Kenya wears a multi-layered beaded necklace with three back pendants indicating her availability for marriage. A Turkana man says of his bride, "It's the things a woman wears that makes her beautiful." This bride carries a fish from Lake Turkana on her head to the family meal. 1986

Page 74 | Richard Evans Schultes | *Río Sucumbios, between Colombia and Ecuador*
The entire adornment of this Kofán shaman—the feathers and necklace, the designs and motifs on the skin—is a conscious attempt to mimic the deportment of the spirit beings encountered after ingesting yagé, or ayahuasca, the most potent psychotropic preparation of the shaman's repertoire. 1941

Page 75 | Carol Beckwith & Angela Fisher | *Niger*
At the annual Geerewol festival, Wodaabe male charm dancers from Niger perform the competitive Yaake dance. The men lighten their skin with yellow powder, accentuate the length of their noses with a line of pigment, and brighten their eyes and teeth with kohl. The men change their facial expressions every few seconds, emphasizing their beautiful teeth and eyes. The winner, in the middle, displays his charisma by holding one eye still while rolling the other from side to side, making him irresistible to the female judges. 1981

Page 76 | Carol Beckwith & Angela Fisher | *Democratic Republic of the Congo*
A chief from the Royal Kuba Kingdom wears a skirt 6 to 9 feet in length, made of hand-woven, palm-fiber cloth panels, gathered around the hips and folded over a belt. With its embroidered overlay and lavish display of palm-fiber tassels, Kuba cloth has been esteemed since the 15th century, and so highly valued that it was once used as currency across much of Central Africa. 2011

Page 77 | Carol Beckwith & Angela Fisher | *Kenya*
To mark his ritual passage from warrior to elder, a Maasai coats his body with a mixture of water and white chalk dug from sources believed to be sacred. With his fingers, he draws decorative patterns, exposing the dark skin below. When he returns home, he must be unrecognizable, especially to his mother. Out of the Eunoto ritual comes anonymity, the basis for his symbolic transition to a new stage of life. 1979

Page 78 | Angela Fisher & Carol Beckwith | *Kenya*
Maasai girls attend the Eunoto ceremony, the ritual that marks the passage of their warrior boyfriends into the rank of elders. Their beaded collars and head-bands are designed to bounce rhythmically, enhancing and accentuating the sensual movements of their bodies. At the Eunoto, each Maasai maiden is allowed to select three from among the warriors. Marriages among the Maasai are typically arranged, but this is the one occasion in a young woman's life when she is free to choose her lovers. 1985

Page 81 | Carol Beckwith & Angela Fisher | *Kenya*
Maasai warriors from Kenya, wearing cloaks of Kanga cloth around their shoulders and framing their faces with ostrich feather headdresses, perform the Enkip-aata dance to horn and voice. They charge wildly around the encampment in small groups, at intervals falling to their knees and waving their headdresses in unison. 1978

Page 82, left | Angela Fisher & Carol Beckwith | *Kenya*
A Samburu warrior from Kenya is expected to be strong, noble and courageous in character, but being Samburu also means he will spend many hours at a time grooming himself. Today, highly sought-after French silk roses, traded in the market, are the pièce de résistance of a warrior's striking coiffure. 2004

Page 82, right | Carol Beckwith & Angela Fisher | *Ghana*
Krobo girls dance at a ceremony marking their initiation into womanhood. This ceremonial passage celebrates their multiple achievements and skills as wives and mothers, trained in the ways of the hearth. 1992

Page 83, left | Angela Fisher & Carol Beckwith | *Danakil Desert, Ethiopia*
An Afar woman, a nomad from the Danakil Desert of Ethiopia, wears amber jewelry and blue veils, dyed with indigo. She exudes a fierce beauty that reflects the challenge of surviving in one of the harshest environments in the world. Traditionally, an Afar warrior who wanted to marry a young girl had to present her with the testicles of his enemy. 1987

Page 83, right | Angela Fisher & Carol Beckwith | *South Sudan*
Dinka men from South Sudan often walk through their cattle camps hand in hand. This physical touching celebrates their close bonds as age-mates. Their tight beaded corsets indicate their position in the age-set system of their tribe. The corsets are first sewn in place at puberty and not removed until the individual reaches a new age set. Each cohort wears a color-coded corset: red and blue for men between the ages of 15 and 25, yellow and blue for men over 30 and ready for marriage. 1979

Page 84 | Angela Fisher & Carol Beckwith | *Ethiopia*
Dassanech men and women walk together in procession around their village during the Dimi ceremony. 2012

Page 85, upper right | Carol Beckwith & Angela Fisher | *Kenya*
A Maasai youth awaits public circumcision at the entrance of a cattle kraal. To numb his senses, his body has been washed with cold water kept overnight in a bucket containing an axe head. 1994

Page 85, lower right | Carol Beckwith & Angela Fisher | *Democratic Republic of the Congo*
A masked dancer emerges from the sacred forest to greet the Kuba Royal Family. The mask is said to represent the strength and grandeur of the Kuba, one of the most enduring living kingdoms of Africa. 2011

Page 86, left | Angela Fisher & Carol Beckwith | *Kenya*
A Pokot girl from Kenya wears a collar necklace of beads cut from the stems of an asparagus tree. Slathered with ocher and oil, the beautiful and dramatic adornment indicates her status as an unmarried girl, open to offers of betrothal. 2003

Page 86, right | Carol Beckwith & Angela Fisher | *Ghana*
The Ashanti Royal Sword Bearer from Ghana wears an eagle-feathered headdress featuring golden ram horns at the Silver Jubilee of the Ashanti King. His role is to protect the King at all ceremonies, warding off evil and absorbing any physical threats to his master. His ritual regalia is believed to protect not only the souls of the royal court but the entire Ashanti nation. 1995

Page 87 | Angela Fisher & Carol Beckwith | *Ethiopia*
Surma men from Ethiopia gather together for one of the wildest sports on the continent, the Donga stick fight. It's designed to settle personal vendettas, prove masculinity and, above all, win wives. There are no rules to the game except that a man must not kill his opponent. If he does, he and his family will be banished for life from the village. 1987

Page 88, upper left | Angela Fisher & Carol Beckwith | *Ethiopia*
Surma girls from Ethiopia paint their faces and bodies with a mixture of chalk and water, highlighting their designs with red ocher. During courtship, their innovative face and body patterns are designed to attract the opposite sex. 1987

Page 88, right | Angela Fisher & Carol Beckwith | *South Sudan*
A Dinka girl from a wealthy family in South Sudan wears a beaded corset to indicate her bride price in cattle. This corset is sewn tightly onto her body and worn until marriage. The height of the beaded projection at the back reveals the wealth of her family and the price for her hand in marriage. This girl's family required 80 head of cattle from her suitor. The devastations of civil war in Sudan and the subsequent infiltration of Christian and Muslim values have made the wearing of corsets a tradition of the past. 1979

Page 88, lower left | Angela Fisher & Carol Beckwith | *Namibia*
On the day of her marriage, a Himba bride from Namibia is surrounded by female relatives who apply a mixture of ocher, aromatic herbs and butterfat to her skin and hide clothing. She wears the traditional Ekori wedding headdress given to her by her mother as a symbol of her status and the treasured conch shell pendant also passed from mother to daughter. 1994

Page 89 | Carol Beckwith & Angela Fisher | *Nigeria*
The Oba, or king, of the Benin Royal Kingdom attends the annual Igue ceremony, which reaffirms the power of the ancient kingdom, and ritually ensures its ongoing prosperity and well-being. Around the king are his royal attendants, including the chief priest, who stands immediately to the right of his sovereign. 2010

Page 90 | Chris Rainier | *Highlands, Papua New Guinea*
Two women are coated with funeral mourning mud, a traditional practice intended to protect the living from dangerous spirits of the dead.

Page 91 | Chris Rainier | *Anguruk area, Highlands, Irian Jaya, New Guinea*
Two Yali warriors with traditional battle penis sheaths and rattan skirts, Anguruk area, Highlands, Irian Jaya, New Guinea

Page 91 | Chris Rainier | *Highlands, NW Irian Jaya, New Guinea*
Four men wear pandanus-leaf rain capes, for protection in a rainstorm.

Page 93 | Chris Rainier | *Sepik River, Papua New Guinea*
A dugout canoe traverses the Sepik River.

Page 94 | Steve McCurry/Magnum Photos | *Larung Gar, near Serthar, Kham, Tibet*
With each prayer, a pilgrim moves closer to his goal, which is not a place but a state of mind, not a destination but a path of liberation. Buddhists spend their time preparing for a moment that we spend most of our lives pretending does not exist—death. We dwell in a whirlwind of activity, racing against time, defining

success by measures of the material world, wealth, power and achievements. This, to the Buddhists, is the essence of ignorance. They remind us that all life grows old and that all possessions decay. Every moment is precious. We all have a choice, to continue on the spinning carousel of delusion, or to step off into a new realm of spiritual possibilities. 2001

Page 97 | Hamid Sardar-Afkhami | *Hovsgol Taiga, Mongolia*
A Duhalar shaman comes out of trance, returning from a healing spiritual journey to the mundane realm of ordinary existence. The shaman is a technician of the sacred. 2001

Page 98 | Carol Beckwith & Angela Fisher | *Ouidah, Benin*
Ewe followers of the powerful deity Koku dance to the rhythm of sacred drums at the King of Voodoo's inauguration in Ouidah, Benin. They wear protective skirts made from the fiber of the alatsi tree, and smear their skin with a paste concocted from palm oil, maize flour and herbs. In West Africa spirit possession is seen as the hand of divine grace. Taken by the spirit, the human becomes the god, and the gods can never be harmed. Believers demonstrate the power of their faith by rolling about on cactus spines or placing burning embers in their mouths with complete impunity. It's an astonishing example of the mind's ability to affect the body that bears it, when catalyzed, in a state of spiritual ecstasy. 2006

Page 99 | Thomas L. Kelly | *Pashupatinath, Kathmandu, Nepal*
Pagalinanda demonstrates the Naga practice of "penis yoga" in his den near the cremation grounds of Pashupatinath. This practice is based on the complete transcendence of sexual impulses, and involves a preliminary nine-year period of self-imposed celibacy. After this, the yogi is truly initiated during a ritual in which certain nerves of the penis are broken, thus enabling him to "lift" rocks weighting over 100 pounds. However, the initiation ceremony for this practice makes it highly unlikely he will ever have another erection. 2001

Page 100 | Chris Rainier | *Timbuktu, Mali*
A Tuareg man reads the Koran in a mosque. In Timbuktu there remains a repository of thousands of ancient manuscripts, dating to a time when the city rivaled Damascus, Baghdad and Cairo as one of the great centers of Islamic culture and learning. One can hold a document embossed in gold and copied in the 13th century from an Avicenna manuscript written in the year 1037.

Page 101 | Hamid Sardar-Afkhami | *Boorqarluk Valley, Hovsgol Taiga, Mongolia*
A Darhat shaman at the end of a healing ceremony suddenly slips back into trance, taken by the spirit. 2008

Page 102 | Brent Stirton/Getty Images | *Rishikesh, India*
Initiates at the Gurukul school of Parmarth Niketan in Rishikesh have their hair shorn as they take the ritual vows and become young monks. All the boys at the school are orphans or come from severely disadvantaged backgrounds. Under the patronage of guru Swami Chidanand Saraswati, a select group will be inducted in the ceremony known as the sacred thread, ritualistically achieving the status of Brahman in the religious order. 2006

Page 103 | Steve McCurry/Magnum Photos | *Haridwar, India*
A young child dressed as the Hindu deity Lord Shiva, often depicted in the color blue, asks for money at a religious festival in Haridwar, India. 1998

Page 104-105 | Chris Rainier | *Lalibella, Ethiopia*
A Coptic priest with cross at a church carved into rock.

Page 106 | James L. Stanfield/National Geographic Stock | *Turkey*
The Mevlevi Sufis are a mystical Islamic order from Turkey, known popularly as the whirling dervishes. They focus all their awareness on God as they spin into trance and attain direct experience of the divine.

Page 107 | Angela Fisher & Carol Beckwith | *Ouidah, Benin*
A Fon voodoo priest carries a pot of flaming embers into the ritual shrine during the coronation of the King of Voodoo in Ouidah, Benin. "Voodoo" is a Fon word that means simply "spirit" or "god." 2006

Page 108-109 | Wade Davis | *Solu Khumbu, Nepal*
Sherab Barma, a traditional Tibetan doctor, whose 7-year training included a 12-month solitary retreat, returns to the cave each year for a month of meditation. Western science, he once remarked, has made a major contribution to minor needs. We spend all of our lifetimes trying to live to be a hundred without losing our hair or teeth. The Buddhist spends his lifetime trying to understand the nature of existence. Billboards in European cities celebrate teenagers in underwear. The Tibetan billboard is the mani wall, mantras carved into stone, prayers for the well-being of all sentient beings. 2005

Page 110 | Gordon Wiltsie | *Baffin Island, Nunavut, Canada*
An Inuit hunter, Jayko Apak, waits for seals on an ice floe. The runners of their sleds were originally made from fish, three Arctic char laid in a row, wrapped in caribou hide and frozen. As hunters, they depend on ice for their survival, and it inspires the very essence of their character and culture. It is the nature of ice, the way it moves, recedes, dissolves and re-forms with the seasons, that gives flexibility to the Inuit heart and spirit. In much of the Arctic, ice once formed in September and remained solid until July. Now it comes in November and is gone by March. The ice is melting, and with it quite possibly a way of life.

Page 113 | Aaron Huey | *Near Manderson, South Dakota*
Riders take a break during a day of war pony races to mark the 1876 defeat of Lt. Col. George Armstrong Custer at the Battle of the Greasy Grass (The Little Big Horn) near Manderson, South Dakota. 2008

Page 114, upper left | Aaron Huey | *South Dakota*
Travis Lone Hill shows tattoos he gave himself at home and in the South Dakota State Prison. He has attempted suicide several times. 2008

173

Page 114, upper right | Aaron Huey | *Near Porcupine, South Dakota*
After intense communication with the spirits, participants - members of the Lakota tribe - emerge from a steaming "inipi," or purification (sweat) lodge. The ceremony pictured here was held by Rick Two Dogs at his home near Porcupine, South Dakota. He is a medicine man descended from American Horse. 2011

Page 114, lower left | Aaron Huey | *Manderson, South Dakota*
A member of the 7th Sign gang is in his room in Manderson, South Dakota, one of the most violent towns on the Pine Ridge Indian Reservation. The home was later condemned, and the family was forced to leave. 2007

Page 114, lower right | Aaron Huey | *South Dakota*
With the reverence afforded a sacred being, Oglala men fell a specially chosen cottonwood tree and carry it to the center of a Sun Dance circle. Erected in the earth, the tree will become the focus of a days-long spiritual ceremony. Sun Dances and other traditional ceremonies have undergone a resurgence since the 1970s.

Page 115 | Aaron Huey | *Oglala, South Dakota*
Stanley Good Voice Elk is a Heyoka (clown dancer) and a dreamer of the Thunder People. His Heyoka name is Wakinyan Hoksila (Wakeeya Hokshila) which means Thunder Boy, or Iktomni Hoksila, Spider Boy. He burns sage, prays and prepares for a coming kettle dance to thank the thunderbeings (thunderstorms) as they leave for the summer. 2011

Page 116, upper left | Wade Davis | *Sarawak, Borneo*
Living in isolation, utterly dependent on the bounty of the forest, the Penan followed the rhythms of the natural world. With no incentive to acquire possessions, they explicitly perceived wealth as the strength of social relations among people. There is no word for "thank you" in their language, for everything is freely given. Hand a cigarette to a Penan woman, and she will tear it apart to distribute the individual strands of tobacco to each hut in the encampment, rendering the product useless but honoring her obligation to share. 1993

Page 116, upper right | David Hiser | *Sarawak, Malaysia*
Asik Nyelit, headman of the Ubong River Penan, was a leader of the Penan resistance. Using blowpipes against bulldozers, the Penan were ultimately no match for the power of the Malaysian state. James Wong, a leading Sarawak politician, remarked, "We don't want them running around like animals. No one has the ethical right to deprive the Penan of the right to assimilation into Malaysian society." 2012

Page 116, lower center | Wade Davis | *Borneo*
To this day the Penan are being overwhelmed by the highest rate of deforestation in the world. Women raised in the forest find themselves working as servants or prostitutes in logging camps that soil every river with debris and silt. Children in government settlement camps succumb to measles and influenza. The basis of the existence of one of the most extraordinary nomadic cultures in the world is being destroyed. Throughout the traditional homeland of the Penan, the sago and rattan, the palms, lianas and fruit trees lie crushed on the forest floor. The hornbill has fled with the pheasant, and as the trees continue to fall, a unique way of life, morally inspired and effortlessly pursued for centuries, has collapsed in a single generation.

Page 117 | David Hiser | *Sarawak, Malaysia*
A Penan family from the Ubong River in Sarawak with a feast of wild foods— sago, wild boar, fruits and seeds—all gathered or hunted in the forest. A Canadian or American grows up believing that poverty for some is a regrettable but inevitable feature of life. The Penan live by the adage that a poor man shames us all. The greatest transgression in their culture is "sihun," a concept that essentially means a failure to share. 2012

Page 118 | Thomas L. Kelly | *Gorotire, Xingu Reserve, Brazilian Amazon*
Sexual activity is regarded among the Kayapo as a natural and desired part of life. Rules regarding such activities are complex and vary between the sexes and different age groups; sexual faithfulness is a matter of individual choice rather than a

common rule. "There are those men who do not like their women to be with someone else; there are others who do not mind," says Kwyra Ka. "Those who do not mind, stay together; those who mind, separate." It is a normal custom for Kayapo Indians to marry, split up and remarry several times. As a rule, chiefs have several sexual partners at the same time.

Page 119 | Thomas L. Kelly | *Humla, Northwest Nepal*
Nyinba women dressed with elaborate turquoise jewelry participate in the polyandry marriage ceremony by dancing and singing as they receive the Nyau, representatives of the groom. Many societies in the Himalaya practice polyandry, with women free to marry several husbands, generally sets of brothers. It is a clever adaptation in lands of sparse resources, as it secures the labor of several men to support a family, even as it limits family size, and thus, the human impact on the environment. But it is also a simple choice, for there are many harsh environments where polyandry is not the norm. Marriage rules are sensitive touchstones of culture. 1986

Page 121 | Richard Evans Schultes | *Rio Pira Parana, Colombia*
An Awayan boy stands in front of a sacred stone decorated with an ancient petroglyph. 1952

Page 122 | Mauricio Lima | *Aral Moreira, Brazil*
A boy plays near a memorial for the late Nisio Gomes, the Guarani leader who was assassinated in November 2011 by masked gunmen, inside the Guaiviry encampment in Aral Moreira, Brazil. 2012

Page 122 | Mauricio Lima | *Aral Moreira, Brazil*
Guarani children play in Aral Moreira, Brazil. 2012

Page 123 | Caroline Bennett | *Rio de Janeiro, Brazil*
Legendary Chief Raoni Metuktire at a peaceful protest outside of UN Rio+20 Earth Summit meetings in Rio de Janeiro, Brazil in July 2012. Raoni is a chief of the Kayapó people, a Brazilian indigenous group from the Mato Grosso and Pará in Brazil south of the Amazon Basin and along Rio Xingu and its tributaries. He has been an international leader in the ongoing struggle against construction of the controversial Belo Monte hydroelectric dam in the heart of the Brazilian Amazon.

Page 124 | AP Photo/William Fernando Martinez | *Outside Toribio, Southern Colombia*
For two generations, Colombia has been convulsed by a violent conflict involving the government, right wing paramilitaries and leftist guerrillas in an open war fueled by the illicit consumption of cocaine. Throughout the nation, indigenous peoples have been caught in the crossfire and they, like all Colombians, have had enough. On July 17, 2012, Nasa Indians assaulted a communication tower manned by six soldiers on the outskirts of Toribio in southern Colombia. They asked only that the security forces and the guerrillas leave their territory, and never return. The soldiers did not resist, and no one was injured. 2012

Page 126 | Brent Stirton/Getty Images | *Loryra, South Omo, Ethiopia*
A Dassanach man tending his fields along the Omo River. A hydroelectric company has plans to construct a massive dam that will inundate much of the Omo Valley, forcibly displacing tribal societies that have lived there for generations."They are cutting down our bush and forest and bulldozing our gardens," an elder laments. "Then they want us to sell off all our cows. No one is going to sell his cattle. They should go away. They should leave our forest alone and leave it to us to cultivate with our hands." 2007

Page 127, upper left | Carol Beckwith & Angela Fisher | *Ethiopia*
The banks of the Omo River in Ethiopia are rich in iron ore deposits and provide a local source of ocher pigment for body painting. Pastoralists by tradition, the Karo people traverse the river daily in dugout canoes to cultivate crops of maize and millet, which supplement their milk diet. 1988

Page 127, upper right | Brent Stirton/Getty Images | *Dilabyno, Omo Valley, Ethiopia*
A number of indigenous peoples of the Omo Valley, including the Beshadar, Hamar and Karo, mark the passage from youth to manhood with a dangerous ritual that excites and galvanizes the entire community. After preliminary preparations and initiations, each boy must leap onto the back of a bull and then run across the herd. Only by doing so does he become a man, empowered by the society to take a bride. 2007

Page 127, lower center | Brent Stirton/Getty Images | *Loryra, South Omo, Ethiopia*
"Our great, great, great grandmothers and grandfathers lived in this land," an elder says of the Dassanech people. "Our fathers lived here, and me, I live here. The men take a fishhook and go to the river and catch a fish and bring it to me to eat. They also go and hunt to bring food for the children. Whose land is this? It belongs to me." 2007

Page 128, upper left | Hamid Sardar-Afkhami | *Olgii Province, Mongolia*
An hunter and his eagle astride his white horse in Mongolia. 2009

Page 128, upper right | Hamid Sardar-Afkhami | *Hovsgol Taiga, Mongolia*
Women heading into a valley to round up the reindeer herds for the evening. 2008

Page 128, lower center | Hamid Sardar-Afkhami | *Hovsgol Taiga, Mongolia*
A boy is caught in deep snow in Mongolia. 2006

Page 129 | Hamid Sardar-Afkhami | *Deloun Highlands, Olgii Province, Outer Mongolia*
Khoda Bergen, a young Kazakh shepherd, is being trained to hunt with his uncle's hunting eagle. 2005

Page 130, upper left | Lynn Johnson | *Guizhou Province, China*
The Dong people are master craftsmen and wood workers. Each settlement has at its heart a tower elaborately constructed from wood, with tight overlapping pagoda-like roofs rising 13 stories to a great signal drum seemingly suspended in the sky. The Dong span their rivers and streams with exquisite wooden bridges, canopies that offer shelter from the wind and rain, and architectural moments that invite contemplation and reflection.

Page 130, lower left | Lynn Johnson | *Guizhou Province, China*
In the Dong culture, parents traditionally, at the time of birth of a child, plant a grove of pines, known as "18 year" trees, which will provide wood for the home of the child and his marriage partner. Death, too, is anticipated. A young girl here shares a laugh with her mother beside her coffin tree, chosen for her at birth. If she follows tradition, she will have the tree cut down and carved to order when she reaches old age. In a sign of the times, one carpentry shop now sells ready-made coffins.

Page 131, upper left | Lynn Johnson | *Guizhou Province, China*
On a trip home to celebrate the New Year, television star Wu Qinglan screens a recent performance for her grandmother. A show she saw as a child on her family's TV, the first in town, inspired her to leave Dimen, the town of her birth, to seek wealth and fame in the city. Out of Dimen's official population of 2,372, about 1,200 work and live elsewhere. The Chinese government actively encourages urban migration, with plans that will bring 300-500 million off the land and into the cities by 2020. Most who find work will end up in factories and assembly plants, earning more than they could in Dimen, but at the sacrifice of all that once embraced them in the quiet mountains of their homeland.

Page 131, upper right | Lynn Johnson | *Guizhou Province, China*
Toughened by a lifetime of fieldwork, the hands of an elderly woman provide loving care for her grandson, who wears a traditional hat adorned in silver. With so many young adults working as migrant laborers, obliged to spend much of their time away in distant cities, the Dong have little choice but to leave child-drearing in the hands of the elderly, creating in effect a culture without mothers or fathers.

Page 131, lower center | Lynn Johnson | *Guizhou Province, China*
Writing is an extraordinary innovation in human history, but it permits and even encourages the numbing of memory. Oral traditions, by contrast, sharpen recollection, even as they seem to open a certain mysterious dialogue with the natural world. Kam, the language of the Dong, has no written form. The history of the culture was traditionally recalled in an epic song composed of some 120 verses. Today, only one woman remembers the entire song. The older women, the za, still sing, passing along knowledge in verse, songs about table manners and field chores, about the moral good of selflessness and the evil of greed.

Page 132 | Steve McCurry/Magnum Photos | *Larung Gar, Kham, Tibet*
The purpose of contemplative practice is to unmask the Buddhanature which – like a buried jewel – shines bright in every human being, waiting to be revealed. Young monk with flowers, Larung Gar, Kham, Tibet. 2000

Page 133, left | Lynn Johnson
The goal of the Chinese Cultural Revolution, unleashed by Mao Zedong in 1966, was to create a pure socialist cadre, men and women whose minds had been purged to yield a template, engraved with the thoughts of Mao. The pursuit of this goal has had tragic consequences. This monk lost his teeth to a cattle prod, one of the many tortures he endured during 18 years in Chinese prisons.

Page 133, right | Lynn Johnson | *Nepal*
The journey through the ice and snow across high passes of the Himalaya to Nepal is fraught with danger. This child survived only because he was carried in the arms of a monk. In the Diamond Sutra, the Buddha cautions that the world is fleeting, like a candle in the wind, a phantom, a dream, the light of stars fading with the dawn. It is upon this insight that Tibetans measure their past and chart their future.

Page 134, left | Lynn Johnson | *Mount Kailash, Nepal*
A father and son circumambulate Mount Kailash before crossing the Himalaya and escaping to exile and freedom in Nepal.

Page 134, right | Steve McCurry/Magnum Photos | *Lhasa, Tibet*
A young Tibetan woman poses next to a Chinese fighter jet on display in front of the Potala Palace, the ancient home of the Dalai Lamas, the spiritual rulers of Tibet. Such symbolic gestures of intimidation are encountered throughout Lhasa. 2000

Page 135 | Lynn Johnson | *Near Mount Kailash, Tibet*
In a village near Kailash, a mountain sacred to Hindu, Buddhist and Jain, a Tibetan cradles a religious relic that he saved from destruction by the Chinese revolutionary cadre. For the Hindu, Kailash is the divine seat of the god Shiva and his wife, the goddess Parvati. For the Tibetan Buddhist, Kailash is remembered for the great Tibetan yogi Milarepa who established homes in the mountains encircling Kailash for 500 Buddhist saints who had achieved enlightenment. Their prayers are still heard by pilgrims who gain spiritual merit by circumambulating the mountain through prostrations, one body length at a time.

Page 137, upper left | Lynn Johnson | *Arunachal Pradesh State, India*
Sunita, aged 3, wears her future dowry, beads inherited through her mother's lineage. Her family speaks Koro Aka, one of hundreds of languages unique to the Indian state of Arunachal Pradesh. Many are on the verge of extinction. One wonders whether young Sunita will still be able to speak her mother tongue by the time she marries and these beads, warm from generations of human touch, pass to the family of her husband.

Page 137, upper right | Lynn Johnson | *California-Nevada border, southeast of Lake Tahoe*
Herman Holbrook, 84, struggled to hold onto his Washoe words until his death in September of last year. As he wandered in the Pine Nut Mountains, where his ancestors had walked for thousands of years, Holbrook explained what the place meant to him: Dik' Ma:sh di ma:sh, or my pine nut lands, my face.

Page 137, lower left | Lynn Johnson | *Sapulpa, Oklahoma*
Maxine Wildcat Barnett, 87, learned Euchee from Grandma Lizzie. But over time her ability to speak her native tongue faded. A devout Methodist, she realized one day that she could no longer sing the praises of Christ in the language of her birth. She began once again to study the language, but was unable to pass it along to her children. Maxine lives alone with her dog, Yahsta. "He understands more Euchee than my kids," she sighs.

Page 137, lower right | Lynn Johnson | *Somes Bar, Northern California*
Charlie "Red Hawk" Thom, 82, is a medicine man and ceremonial leader. English, he says, goes in one ear and out the other; it never touches the heart. His native Karuk, by contrast, begins in the heart and moves to the mind. To say you love something, you say ick-ship-eee-mihni. "If you tell a woman eee-mihni" he says, "well, you'd better be ready to marry her."

Page 138 | Brent Stirton/Getty Images | *Kalahari Desert, Namibia/South Africa*
In the Kalahari, a San elder crosses a fence marking land claimed by a mining company. Until the early years of the 20th century, when the impact of alcohol and resettlement camps and the false and twisted promises of development shattered many of their lives, the San had followed the rhythm of their natural world. Today, they are marginalized in their own homeland, with many forced to live in government resettlement camps. 2006

Page 140 | James P. Blair/National Geographic Stock | *Serra Pelada, Brazil*
A booming, makeshift gold mine in Brazil is carved out of a former rainforest.

Page 142 | Steve McCurry/Magnum Photos | *Mumbai, India*
A woman carrying metal lunch boxes walks past hundreds of men in prayer. Women, it is famously said, hold up half of the sky. Throughout the world, they also do much of the work, even as they have primary responsibility for the day-to-day well-being of their children. Globalization, which has drawn millions of women into assembly plants, working long hours for nominal pay, has not eased the burden of the mothers of the world. 1996

Page 144 | Randy Olson, OlsonFarlow.com | *Easther Beijing, Tongzhou District, China*
Young women from the country train to be servants at the Fuping Vocational Skills Training School in Beijing. 2005

Page 145 | Edward Burtynsky | *Dehui City, Jilin Province, China*
The Deda Chicken Processing Plant in China. 2005

Page 146 | A Yin | *Xilinhaote City, Inner Mongolia*
Saihandeliger was born December 30, 1998, in a small Mongolian village some 90 miles from Xilinhaote, the town where she now goes to school. Her parents are poor herders who manage 5,000 acres of pastureland for the owner. Saihandeliger lives with relatives. She attends Class 3 of Grade 4 of No. 6 Primary School. The first image was taken in February 2008, the second in June 2010.

Page 148 | A Yin | *Wuzhumuqing Banner, Inner Mongolia*
Wurentana was born April 19, 2004. Her parents are poor herders, managing but 800 acres for an absentee owner. Wurentana lives with her grandmother and studies in preschool class 3 of No. 2 Mongolian Primary School in Wuzhumuqing Banner, 80 miles from her home. The first image was taken in December 2008, the second in June 2010.

Page 149 | A Yin | *West Dongzhumuqing Banner, Inner Mongolia*
Sulide was born May 19, 2005. His parents were herders, but the desertification of the lands they once managed forced them to move to town to find work in 2009. His father is a maintenance worker and his mother has a job in a modest restaurant. Sulide attends kindergarten and is a member of its senior class. The first image was taken in December 2005, the second in June 2010.

Page 151 | A Yin | *Wuzhumuqing Banner, Inner Mongolia*
Wendusubatu was born September 16, 2004. His parents do relatively well, managing as herders 12,600 acres of meadow and grasslands. Wendusubatu lives with his grandparents 100 miles away while he attends the middle class of kindergarten. The first image was taken in May 2005, the second in July 2010.

Page 152 | Steve McCurry/Magnum Photos | *Rangoon, Myanmar*
A procession of Nuns in Rangoon, Myanmar (Burma). 1994

Page 155 | Steve McCurry/Magnum Photos | *Rajasthan, India*
A young woman enjoys time with her family after the monsoons in Rajasthan. 1983

Page 156 | Brent Stirton/Getty Images | *Lake Murray, Western Province, Papua New Guinea*
Kubut children launch themselves into the waters of Lake Murray in the western highlands of Papua New Guinea. 2008

Page 157 | Timothy Allen | *Papua New Guinea*
Members of the Huli tribe dance at a Sing Sing. Celebrated throughout the high-lands of New Guinea, these great ritual gatherings bring together many tribes, allowing each to flaunt its cultural brilliance in dance, finery and song.

Page 158 | Steve McCurry/Magnum Photos | *Bangladesh*
Children swim along the Dhaka-Chittagong rail line in Bangladesh. 1982

Page 160 | Steve McCurry/Magnum Photos | *Haridwar, India*
A Naga Sadhu sits surrounded by his religious items during the Kumbh Mela Festival in Haridwar, India. 2010

Page 161 | Steve McCurry/Magnum Photos | *Mumbai, India*
A group of men at one of Mumbai's 37 laughing clubs. 1996

Page 163 | Steve McCurry/Magnum Photos | *Henan Province, China*
Monks in training practice martial arts at the Shaolin Monastery in Henan Province, China. 2004